Let's Make

Bread

by Mari Bolte

NORWOOD HOUSE  PRESS

Norwood House Press

For information regarding Norwood House Press, please visit our website at:
www.norwoodhousepress.com or call 866-565-2900.

PHOTO CREDITS: page 4: ©JGI/Jamie Grill / Getty Images; page 7: ©nutsiam / Shutterstock; page 8: ©Roshianu and moloko / Shutterstock; page 11: ©Irina Fischer / Shutterstock; page 12: ©sasimoto / Shutterstock; page 15: ©pic0000 / Shutterstock; page 16: ©PonyWang / Getty Images; page 19: ©Rosa Herrara; page 21: ©Rosa Herrara; page 22: ©Rosa Herrara; page 23: ©Rosa Herrara; page 24: ©Rosa Herrara page 27: ©Rosa Herrara; page 28: ©Rosa Herrara

Hardcover ISBN: 978-1-68450-778-8
Paperback ISBN: 978-1-68404-753-6

LIBRARY OF CONGRESS CATALOGING-IN-PUBLICATION DATA
Library of Congress Cataloging-in-Publication Data has been filed and is available at catalog.loc.gov

353N—082022
Manufactured in the United States of America in North Mankato, Minnesota.

Contents

Bread is a mixture of flour, water, and an ingredient that helps the dough expand.

CHAPTER 1

All about Bread

People have been making bread for tens of thousands of years. It is eaten around the world. Flour is bread's main ingredient. Growing and collecting **grains** to turn into flour used to be hard work. Imagine gathering tiny grains of wheat and then spending hours grinding them into powder!

At first, people might have gathered wheat as they moved from one place to another. When they started making permanent homes and growing crops, bread became an everyday food.

Scientists have found evidence of ground grain from 22,000 years ago. People in Israel made flat cakes of seeds and grains. They heated them over a fire. Some people still use this method today.

The first people to farm the land lived in the Middle East. They grew barley for bread. Cities popped up around farms. Places to store extra grain were built. The extra grain could be traded or saved for later.

The first **yeast** bread dates back to ancient Egypt. Yeast is a kind of living **microbe**. It has been around for hundreds of millions of years! Yeast allows bread to **rise** and be airy inside.

Yeast needs to be fed and kept alive. Bakers discovered that saving a bit of dough from one batch helped the next one rise.

Some of the first bread ovens were made of clay.

Some people took it a step further and created a **starter**. They kept their yeast dough alive in a jar and fed it flour. Then, they used a bit to start their next batch. The starter was called **sourdough**. Sourdough starters take a little longer to rise. They also give the bread a tangy flavor.

Bread-slicing machines make uniform slices.

Miners brought sourdough starters along during the California Gold Rush in 1848. Legend says the miners cuddled with their sourdough starters at night to keep the starters warm.

In 1868, Charles and Maximilian Fleischmann began selling cakes of yeast. The cakes needed to be kept cool. They lived for about two weeks. People did not need to feed sourdough starters to make bread at home anymore.

Today, Fleischmann sells several kinds of yeast. You may recognize their packets or jars of yeast in the baking aisle of your grocery store. Professional bakers still use yeast cakes.

For thousands of years, people had to slice their own bread. A sharp knife was needed. Slices were not always the same size. The first sliced bread was sold by the Chillicothe Baking Company in 1928.

Inventor Otto Rohwedder made a machine. It sliced bread and then wrapped it in wax paper. A baker figured out that keeping the slices together and putting them in a tin kept the bread fresher for longer.

A few years later, Wonder Bread started selling sliced bread around the country.

There are many kinds of bread. Most people think of crusty loaves or soft bread used for sandwiches. Both use wheat flour. There are many other options. People on gluten-free diets use rice, almond, buckwheat, or other wheat-free flour. Quick breads, like banana or corn bread, don't require yeast. The dough does not need to be **kneaded** either. Kneading activates gluten, a **protein** found in flour. The gluten expands when the bread rises. The proteins make the dough elastic.

People like to butter their bread. They also like to spread on jelly, nut butter, or honey. Bread is toasted, grilled, and stacked. Sandwiches are nothing without delicious bread!

In the United States, the average person eats about 50 loaves of bread a year. A loaf of sliced bread has between 20 and 24 slices. That's a lot of sandwiches!

Parts of Bread

Crust

Toppings

12

While there are more than 500 different species of yeast, only one is used in modern baking.

CHAPTER 2

Make Your Own Bread

Leavened bread wouldn't be what it is without yeast. Most yeast is sold in envelopes. When you open one and pour it out, you'll see little brown grains. In that tiny palmful of grains, there are more than 200 billion yeast **cells**. And each one is alive! They have been partially dehydrated so they go **dormant**.

Yeast can be activated with warm liquid. Water can be used. A mix of milk and water will make a softer loaf. Are you hungry after waking up from a long nap? So is yeast. Yeast like to eat sugar as a tasty snack! The microbes eat the sugar and burp out bubbles of gas. The gas is made of carbon dioxide.

Once your yeast is fed, it's time to add flour. Kneading the dough helps all the ingredients mix in evenly. It also helps develop the springy, airy, chewy inside of the bread.

Bread machines can knead for you. But it's easy to do by hand too. Just fold the dough in half. Then, press it down with the heel of your hand. Keep doing this until the dough is stretchy and elastic.

Lots of kneading and good yeast action create many large holes in the bread, called an open crumb.

The bubbles created by the yeast stretch the dough like a balloon. The stretchier the dough, the bigger the bubbles can be. Kneading distributes the bubbles evenly.

Letting dough rest is just as important as kneading. Bread usually gets two resting periods—after kneading and before baking. Resting lets the proteins relax back into their proper shapes. Not resting can result in heavy, tough bread.

As bread dough bakes, the gas bubbles grow. The liquid heats up and evaporates too. This rise is called oven spring. When this stage is complete, the crust begins to bake and get crisp. The yeast dies off. The gas pressure builds in the dough, making the bubbly holes in the baked bread.

When your bread is baked through, it will make a hollow sound when you tap it. If you're not sure, use a food thermometer. The center of the loaf should be 212° Fahrenheit (100° Celsius).

It will be tempting to cut into your warm loaf. But bread is best when it is allowed to rest for at least 20 to 45 minutes. Even after coming out of the oven, your bread is losing moisture. This dries the inside of the bread and makes it firm.

Always have an adult help with putting baked goods into the oven, and taking them back out!

If you cut a warm loaf, the inside of the bread might be gummy or doughy. Then, as steam escapes, the bread will get dry faster than usual.

Let bread cool completely at room temperature. Then, you can store it for future eating. Paper bags will ensure your bread stays crusty. Paper lets air flow through. The loaf will dry out fast, though.

Keeping the loaf in a plastic bag or wrapped in foil will hold in moisture. However, moisture can also cause mold to grow. Freezing is another option. Slice your loaf before freezing. Let it defrost in the refrigerator, unwrapped, overnight to prevent a soggy slice.

However you store it, it's best to eat fresh bread within a few days. It will be so tasty, your bread probably won't last long enough to grow mold!

Materials Checklist

- ✓ 2/3 cup white sugar
- ✓ large bowl
- ✓ 1 cup warm water
- ✓ 1 cup warm milk (if dairy-free, use water or almond milk)
- ✓ large mixing spoon
- ✓ 0.25-gram envelope of yeast (2 1/4 teaspoons)

- ✓ 5 1/2 cups bread flour or gluten-free flour blend
- ✓ 1 1/2 teaspoons salt
- ✓ 1/4 cup vegetable oil plus extra for greasing
- ✓ measuring cups
- ✓ sharp knife
- ✓ loaf pans

Hot liquid can kill yeast. Test the liquid with your finger. If it feels just slightly warm, it's perfect.

CHAPTER 3

In the Kitchen!

Now that you know what goes into bread, it's time to make your own!

1. Pour the sugar into a bowl. Add the warm water and milk. Stir to combine.

2. Stir in the yeast.

3. Set the bowl aside for about 10 minutes until the yeast gets foamy. If your yeast doesn't foam, check the expiration date on the package. If your yeast has expired, start again with fresh yeast.

For accuracy, be sure to use dry measuring cups for the flour!

4. Add 1 cup of flour to the bowl.

5. Add salt and vegetable oil. Stir until everything is combined.

6. Stir in as much of the remaining flour as you can. It's going to be hard work!

24

7. Turn the dough out onto a floured surface. Knead for 10 minutes, adding the rest of the flour as you knead. Now, the dough should be smooth and elastic.

8. Pour a little oil into the bowl. Use your hand to gently spread the oil along the bottom and sides. Then, place the dough in the bowl.

9. Cover and set in a warm place until it has doubled in size. This will take about an hour, depending on how warm the room is.

10. Remove the dough from the bowl. Knead it for three minutes. Ask an adult to cut it in half.

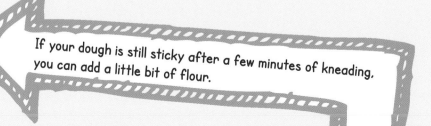

If your dough is still sticky after a few minutes of kneading, you can add a little bit of flour.

11. Shape the dough into two loaves. Place them in greased loaf pans.

12. Let the loaves rise for 30 minutes. Partway through, preheat the oven to 350 degrees.

13. With an adult's help, bake for 30 minutes. When the loaves are done, they will be golden brown on top and sound hollow when you tap them.

14. Let the loaves cool for at least 10 minutes before carefully turning them out of the pans.

15. Once your loaves are completely cool, slice your bread. Enjoy your fresh bread with butter, jam, or sandwich fixings!

Your hard work of measuring, mixing, and kneading has paid off. You can continue to grow your baking skills by trying this recipe again or trying new ones!

Bake It Better!

Congratulations! You have made bread. Now see if there are ways to make it even better. Use any of these changes and see how they improve your bread.

- After step 7, mix in 2 cups of dried fruit, chocolate chips, or nuts. Then proceed with step 8.

- During step 10, divide dough into 12 rolls instead of 2 loaves. Check the rolls after 10 minutes in the oven.

- During step 11, after the loaves are shaped, brush with oil or melted butter. Sprinkle sesame, flax, poppy, or sunflower seeds on top. You can also sprinkle on shredded cheese or rolled oats.

Glossary

cells (SELLZ): the smallest units of a living thing

dormant (DOOR-muhnt): inactive

grains (GRAYNZ): the fruit or seeds of a cereal crop, such as wheat

kneaded (NEE-ded): squeezed and folded together, usually by hand

leavened (LEV-uhnd): being made to rise with the addition of a substance, such as yeast

microbe (MY-krohb): an organism made up of only one cell

protein (PRO-teenz): a complex molecule that provides structure and support to cells

rise (RYS): the stage in breadmaking where dough is left to rest and double in size

sourdough (SOW-uhr-doh): dough left over from a previous batch of bread and used in the next batch

starter (STAR-tuhr): a mixture of yeast and good bacteria that eats flour

yeast (YEEST): a single-celled microbe that expels carbon dioxide as waste

For More Information

Books

Atherton, David. *Bake, Make, and Learn to Cook: Fun and Healthy Recipes for Young Cooks*. Somerville, MA: Candlewick Press, 2021.

Biberdorf, Kate. *Kate the Chemist: The Awesome Book of Edible Experiments for Kids*. New York, NY: Philomel Books, 2021.

Shaw, Katie. *Bread Baking for Teens: 30 Step-by-Step Recipes for Beginners*. Emeryville, CA: Rockridge Press, 2021.

Websites

Britannica Kids (https://kids.britannica.com/students/article/bread/273343) Learn the history behind the "stuff of life."

Foodlets (https://foodlets.com/2018/10/22/the-easy-bread-recipe-your-kids-can-make-themselves/) An easy homemade bread recipe that kids can make.

Science Sparks (https://www.science-sparks.com/science-sparks-bake-off/) Learn about baking—while making! Baking challenges teach delicious lessons.

Index

About the Author

Mari Bolte has worked in publishing as a writer and editor for more than 15 years. She has written dozens of books about things like science and craft projects, historical figures and events, and pop culture. She lives in Minnesota.